'Future generations will wo [illegible] amazement that the early twenty-first century's developed world went into hysterical panic over a globally average temperature increase of a few tenths of a degree, and, on the basis of gross exaggerations of highly uncertain computer projections combined into implausible chains of inference, proceeded to contemplate a rollback of the industrial age.'

Richard Lindzen, retired Professor of Atmospheric Physics at MIT

All you need to know about Climate Change

... in cartoons

Cartoons by Josh

All you need to know about Climate Change... in cartoons
Climategate 10th Anniversary Edition

www.cartoonsbyjosh.com

First published in November 2019

ISBN 978-0-9550059-8-5

Published by Cartoons by Josh

For Christopher Booker

Christopher Booker, the superb writer and journalist who died recently, was a wonderful encourager, friend and mentor. He was particularly encouraging of this book of cartoons. I include these kind words he wrote some years ago.

'For all of us involved in the deadly serious, incredibly complex and suffocatingly technical debate over climate change, Josh has performed a unique service. His brilliant cartoons have sent constant little shafts of light through the fog. He follows the arguments, he knows the names, he draws like a dream and he makes us laugh.

In a world where we are expected to take charlatans like Al Gore, James Hansen, Michael Mann, Lord Deben and Ed Davey seriously, his deftly witty comments put it all in blessed perspective, in a way for which we are all in his debt.'

I dedicate this book to him.

Peer reviewed cartoons

Foreword

There is a lot wrong with the world, but a lot right too. Compared with when I was born, the world has more green vegetation, more whales, polar bears, wolves, ospreys, eagles and beavers, cleaner rivers, lower child mortality, less poverty, fewer wars, milder winters, slightly fewer droughts and far fewer deaths from famines, floods and storms. Yet we are told that we must panic, despair and deliberately impose harsh austerity on ordinary people just in case the current gentle warming of the climate turns nasty at some point later in the century. And anybody who dissents from this is immediately labelled a heartless and evil crank. How did that come about?

Nobody does a better job of exposing with wit the shaky foundations on which these predictions of doom are built than Josh. In these pages are real scientific, economic and political arguments expressed in ingenious cartoons, their background explained in paragraphs of pithy text. I plan to put a copy of this book in a drawer, in an envelope addressed to a putative grandchild, with written on it: "Do not open till the year 2050". If the grandchild opens it while gnawing on a human bone in a ruined hovel in a desert landscape, then the alarmists were right. If instead he or she is living amidst plenty in a cleaner, greener world, then Josh will have been right to poke fun at the gloomsters of today.

Matt Ridley

UNBALANCED

A TALE OF TWO PLATFORMS

JONATHAN PORRITT & CAROLINE LUCAS DON'T WANT TO TALK TO CLIMATE CHANGE SCEPTICS. THE FEELING IS MUTUAL.

A group of activists and environmentalists wrote an open letter saying that climate change sceptics should not be allowed to air their views in public. Why? We often hear 'The debate is over.' But when did we have it? Was it in public or behind closed doors? Is there any record of this great debate?

Why Climate Change?

A decade ago I became intrigued by a news story called 'Climategate'.

There was little coverage in the mainstream media for what was clearly a major exposé of possible data manipulation by a small but influential group of climatologists. The leaker, who called himself Mr FOIA, released the emails because he wanted to blow the whistle on the state of climate science (you can read his full explanation at the end of this book). The emails showed the scientists to be attempting to manufacture an alarming narrative with uncertain and heavily adjusted data while blocking anyone who disagreed with them or might find something wrong with it. Despite the topic supposedly concerning a possible manmade planetary catastrophe, most journalists ignored or played down the story. If you wanted to read more then the best place was on Internet blogs.

The blogs were a revelation to me – so many articulate discussions analysing and dissecting the science, the alarm and the politics.

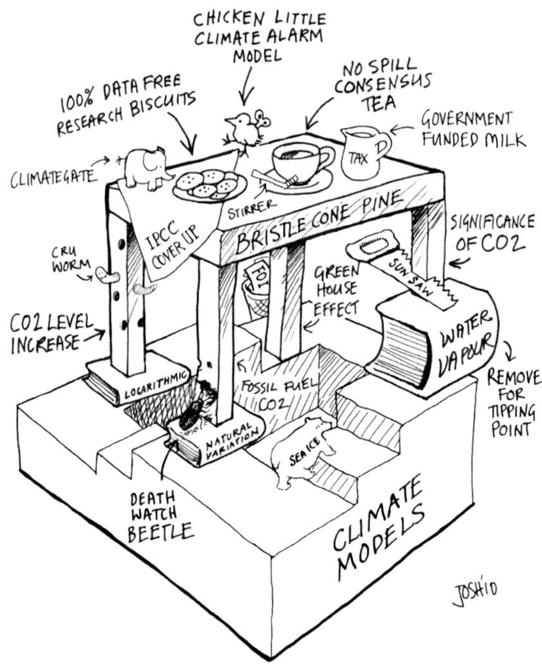

The complicated world of climate science

The problem, I soon discovered, was that the science of climate change is complex and diverse. While the consensus alarmist position was, and still is, well funded, widely promoted, with easy-to-access, seemingly reliable sources of information, the counterarguments were much harder to find. The topic requires reading widely and, in the process, probably marking oneself as a politically incorrect social pariah. It still feels dangerous to ask questions or even contemplate an alternate narrative – maybe even to read this book.

My thought ten years ago was that the topic was ripe for satire and helpful visual explainers. Here was the greatest threat facing mankind, with attendant celebrities, activists and politicians, but based on suspiciously flaky foundations.

ALARMIST

IT'S ON THE T.V. IT MUST BE TRUE!

FAKE NEWS

ALARMED

SKEPTIC

WOW, THEY DON'T ACTUALLY KNOW..

GLOBAL WARMING

CONCERNED

DON'T WORRY! I'VE JUST BEEN PHOTOSHOPPED

CAUTIOUS

I'M SO GLAD I DIDN'T BUY A DIESEL LIKE THE ENVIRONMENTALISTS TOLD ME TO

DISENGAGED

THEY'VE ADJUSTED THE TEMPERATURES AGAIN?!?

DOUBTFUL

THANK GOODNESS FOR FOSSIL FUELS GIVING US CHEAP ENERGY FOR HEALTH, WEALTH + EDUCATION!

GAS

DISMISSIVE

JOSH '18
WITH APOLOGIES TO MICHAEL SLOAN

THE 'SIX AMERICAS' FRAMEWORK IS BEING USED BY CLIMATE EDUCATORS + COMMUNICATORS

Above: A spoof of an illustration which identifies different audiences and how to communicate climate change to them. I have concluded most of us are sceptics.

Below: how much temperature rise is due to poor siting of thermometers?

Through the climate blogosphere I met Andrew Montford, who was, at the time, publishing a book called *The Hockey Stick Illusion,* and he encouraged me to draw cartoons to post on his blog. His book, by the way, is a superb detective dissection of the infamous 'Hockey Stick' global temperatures graph and a great read.

This book takes a simple format – an illustrated narrative on the right-hand page with more cartoons and captions on the left-hand page. It's short and hopefully a resource and springboard to further reading and making up your own mind. The cartoons represent the past ten years of reading and listening, attending conferences and lectures. They might not persuade one way or the other but I hope they help the discussion.

I don't try to cover every aspect of the science or to try to explain everything in minute detail as I have come to believe that is not 'All you need to know'.

POLAR BEARS THRIVING
CLIMATE SCIENCE FACING EXTINCTION

Polar bears are iconic climate change alarmist mascots. Fortunately, they are thriving.

BIOFUELS
POLITICS
ACTIVISM
ALARMISM
SCIEN2
FAKE DATA
JOSH'18
CASH
GRANTS
MONEY
SUBSIDIES
PHYSICS
SCIENCE
WEATHER
DATA
STATISTICS
PALEO STUDIES
ANALYSIS
CLIMATE

Confronting Complexity

'Climate science' is a raft of many subjects and disciplines, including atmospheric physics and chemistry, weather systems and meteorology, geology, solar physics, soil science, glaciology, oceanography, data gathering and statistical analysis, computer science, mathematical modelling, time series analysis, biological sciences, and studies of past climate – and many more.

Some climate scientists gather data, others analyse the data. The first group might travel to the Arctic and send back pictures of stunning icy blue and white landscapes, plus polar bears. The second lot sit in darkened rooms in front of computer screens, creating computer models and alarming predictions.

Alongside the sciences there's the politics, activism and environmentalism and, of course, billions and billions of dollars in energy taxes, grants, subsidies and 'green finance'.

Trying to understand any of it is a challenge, but if climate change is going to be a catastrophe and we are to blame, then we should all try to grasp something of its implications. Vast resources of time and money – yours – are currently being spent trying to tackle it and there is political pressure to alter our lifestyles, introduce global treaties and change current economic models.

In every corner of climate change there are strongly expressed opinions and beliefs – even the science is a war zone. The vitriol poured out on blogs and social media is astonishing, even, dare I say it, alarming. The Climategate emails exposed lies, deception and exaggeration that should not go unchallenged.

Truth, however you discover it, is vital - without it we are lost. The science isn't settled; it has hardly begun. Although my medium is cartoons, it is, of course, a serious debate.

The cartoon opposite shows how I felt battling a many-snake-headed-tangled-rooted monster. There are so many conflicting and powerful factions to grapple with. Why is so much data secret or adjusted? Why are renewable subsidies so huge? Who is getting the cash (not climate sceptics, that's for sure)? Why is it so political?

We all need to fight the monster, to discover what we can safely ignore, what we should pay attention, to learn and act on.

Let's start where many people start and take a look at the science. It is after all, why some believe there is a problem in the first place.

NURSING THE STATISTICS BACK TO HEALTH

Sir Paul Nurse, the UK geneticist cartooned here, made fundamental errors in a BBC programme on climate change. Correcting them allows us to look at the annual amounts of manmade CO_2 emissions which are tiny compared to natural CO_2 emissions and compared to the main greenhouse gas which is water vapour. CO_2 has a logarithmic or diminishing effect on climate forcing.

Although the levels of CO_2 in the atmosphere are a focus for climate science it is the feedbacks which are crucial to the 'alarm'. Only if there are large positive feedbacks is there any problem with increasing CO_2. And it looks like feedbacks are small. We know, because we are still here, that the planet is able to cope with much higher levels than our present low levels of CO_2.

The Science – CO_2

Is the climate changing at all, does mankind have any influence on it and will burning fossil fuels and emitting CO_2 warm the planet?

It looks like we can say 'yes' to those questions. Yes, the climate of Planet Earth has changed in the last 100 years – it has warmed to a degree (pun intended). And, yes, burning fossil fuels does release CO_2 , a so-called 'greenhouse' gas, into the atmosphere and, scientists believe, this should have the effect of warming the atmosphere. Deforestation, urbanisation, land use and other factors also have an effect on climate so, yes, man's activities do and will continue to have an effect now and in the future. This part of the debate is not controversial.

How big or catastrophic this effect is or will be is uncertain. In the meantime, climate change science and activists have focused on CO_2 as being the main driver of climate which, given the annual amounts of manmade emissions (see opposite), is a bit of a puzzle.

CLIMATE CONTROL KNOBS

CLIMATE SCIENTISTS DISCOVER THAT OCEANS HAVE A MAJOR INFLUENCE* ON GLOBAL TEMPERATURES

* "WE TOLD YOU SO" BY A.N. SCEPTIC

We crave certainty and the media are happy to sell it to us. But when it comes to the climate it isn't there. It's chaotic yet stable. In the above cartoon Richard Betts of the Met Office points out that one source, soil, emits much more CO_2 than we do, a ratio of 60:8.

When you look at 'The Science' you come to the following conclusion: we know very little. The data is incomplete, uncertain and so continuously adjusted that it is and might always be unreliable, particularly if, as it seems, the data is being manipulated for political and economic ends. Tony Heller, who blogs at Real Climate Science, has been documenting the manipulation of temperature data for many years.

Other scientific studies do show the planet has warmed, from shrinking glaciers and a decrease in summer Arctic sea ice, to changes in vegetation and sea-level rise. As the Intergovernmental Panel on Climate Change, or IPCC, says 'Scientific evidence for warming of the climate system is unequivocal.' But there are no observational scientific studies that show that the warming is due to the CO_2 emissions which come from fossil fuels. None. Zip. Nada.

The best that 'The Science' can do is infer that this might be a possibility because when they try to model the climate on computers they cannot explain the recent modern warming without adding in a CO_2 emissions 'parameter'.

So drastic changes to global economies are being proposed because of computer model projections.

FRANKENSCIENCE

OF THE CLIMATE KIND

The Science – Uncertainty

Uncertainty dominates climate science – a scrapbook of computer analysis, atmospheric physics, paleoscience, earth and biological sciences, maths and statistics. And yet still manages to leave huge areas of science out.

As I have already noted, a good example of uncertainty is the actual temperature of the planet. Scientists, year on year, adjust the raw temperature data and come up with new trends. If you continually adjust the past, for whatever reason, it will always be a moving target and an interpretation. So how will we ever know?

That is worth repeating. We will probably never reliably or accurately know what the global temperature is or ever was.

The rot set in some time ago, and goes back thousands of years – cue 'The Hockey Stick'.

Right: Yamal refers to a significant tree in a study similar to the Hockey Stick graph. The tree ring data from this one tree gave the graph a cool medieval period. Just one tree.

ONCE YOU'VE SEEN ONE TREE
YOU'VE SEEN YAMAL

Below: Steig, Gergis and Marcott are climate scientists. 'Lew' refers to Stephan Lewandowsky , a social scientist who believes fervently in conspiracies. Cook is an Australian blogger.

ROTTEN TO THE CORE

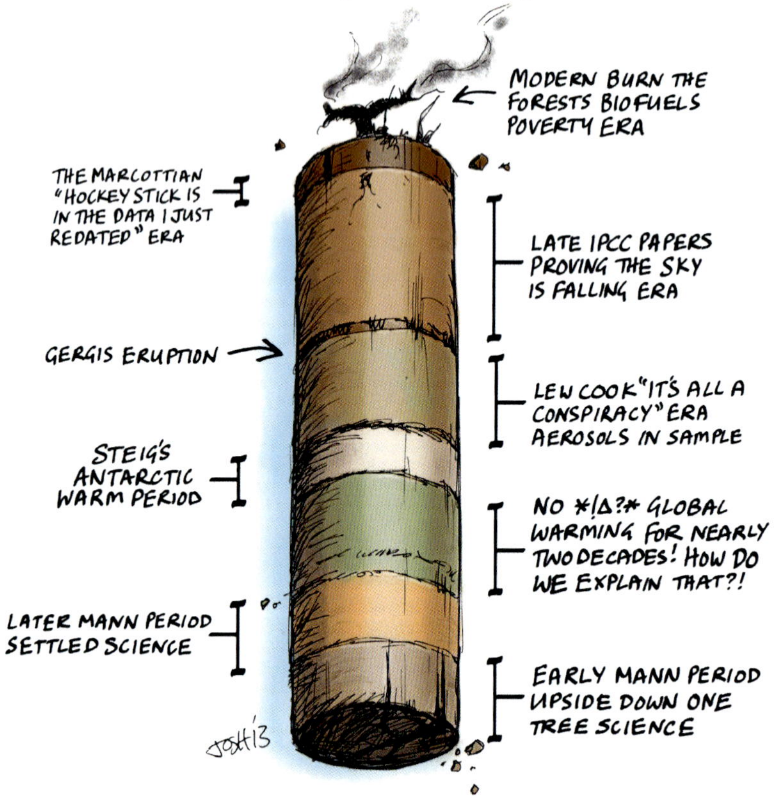

MODERN BURN THE FORESTS BIOFUELS POVERTY ERA

THE MARCOTTIAN "HOCKEY STICK IS IN THE DATA I JUST REDATED" ERA

LATE IPCC PAPERS PROVING THE SKY IS FALLING ERA

GERGIS ERUPTION

LEW COOK "IT'S ALL A CONSPIRACY" ERA AEROSOLS IN SAMPLE

STEIG'S ANTARCTIC WARM PERIOD

NO *!Δ?* GLOBAL WARMING FOR NEARLY TWO DECADES! HOW DO WE EXPLAIN THAT?!

LATER MANN PERIOD SETTLED SCIENCE

EARLY MANN PERIOD UPSIDE DOWN ONE TREE SCIENCE

JOSH '13

THE CURRENT STATE OF PALEO CLIMATE SCIENCE

The Science – The Hockey Stick

Andrew Montford's book, the previously mentioned *The Hockey Stick Illusion,* details how Steve McIntyre and Ross McKitrick challenged the so-called 'Hockey Stick' graph of past global temperatures created by climate scientists, notably Michael Mann of Penn State University.

Mann's graph showed 20th century temperature as 'unprecedented' in the last 1000 years but Steve and Ross showed the graph was bogus and based on dodgy data and biased mathematics and some famously inaccurate tree rings, used as a proxy for past temperatures.

Thankfully, because of these criticisms, climate science has, more or less, ditched the 'Hockey Stick' and the idea that 20th century warming is unusual. They have returned to Hubert Lamb's graph showing the Medieval Warm Period and the Little Ice Age and which forms the outline of the hills in the cartoon below.

Data suggests it was hotter then, globally and with rates of warming just as fast as today. We cannot know for certain, of course – nothing in climate science is – but it looks like both the rate and degree of present day warming is not unusual.

The reference to Sheep Mountain is the location of some of the tree ring samples and, of course, makes for a nice allusion to the temperature graph by Hubert Lamb, the famous British climatologist.

THE THREE STOOGES

Left: the three UK inquiries into Climategate, were led by Sir Russell Muir, Lord Oxburgh and the UK Parliament. The third stooge shown is Lord Acton, the vice chancellor of the University of East Anglia where the climatologists at the Climate Research Unit were based.

The inquires did nothing to restore trust in climate science, if anything they made it worse. Their failure led to ongoing climate grief, see below.

The Science – Climategate

Mann and the other paleoclimatologists who were behind the Hockey Stick graph, were also at the heart of the 'Climategate', scandal, mentioned at the start. It was bad enough to lead to several official UK inquiries.

One was set the task of looking into the science but reported back that it didn't look into the science. Another allowed the university to set the scope of the inquiry.

There was a collective establishment shrug of the shoulders. Despite this, Climategate had exposed and confirmed climate science as weak and uncertain. The consequence for science as a whole is that there has been a decrease in trust. In a 2012 report 'Climate Science, The Public and the News media', 51% of those surveyed said they trusted scientists, but only 38% said they trusted climate scientists. The public simply do not find climate science credible.

Here might be why, an email* from 2005: 'For much of the SH (Southern Hemisphere) between 40 and 60S the normals are mostly made up as there is very little ship data there.' So when they don't have actual data they just make it up?

Here's another: 'Lowering the pre-instrumental temperatures in the Southern Hemisphere by about 0.2^{o}C would thus further strengthen the case for human-induced warming during the 20th century.' So if the data doesn't quite fit the story, they change the data?

A third: 'The two MMs [McIntyre and McKitrick] have been after the CRU station data for years. If they ever hear there is a Freedom of Information Act now in the UK, I think I'll delete the file rather than send to anyone. ' Delete the data to avoid letting someone see it?

Let's look at one email in particular, the infamous 'trick... to hide the decline'.

**A link to all the Climategate emails is at the end of the book.*

MIKE'S NATURE TRICK TO HIDE THE DECLINE

Above: drawn to clarify 'Hide the decline' to Scott Adams, bestselling author, cartoonist and creator of the Dilbert comic strip. He has recently become interested in the climate change debate from a 'persuasion' point of view.

Below: my take on 'The Consensus'. It cannot exist in any meaningful way if no scientist knows what other scientists measure or how they analyse it.

NO TRANSPARENCY NO CONSENSUS

The Science – Hiding It

'Mike's Nature trick... to hide the decline' is one of the most notorious and damaging exchanges from the Climategate emails. Happily, it is a fairly straightforward bit of science.

Here is the whole quote: 'I've just completed Mike's Nature trick of adding in the real temps to each series for the last 20 years (i.e., from 1981 onwards) and from 1961 for Keith's to hide the decline.'

Mike, and his fellow climate scientists, knew that some of the tree ring data, used for the hockey stick graph, showed a decrease in temperatures in the last few decades while actual thermometer data showed a warming trend. So the two sets of data contradicted each other. This problem, well known in climate science, was called 'the divergence problem.' Unfortunately they tried to hide the problem. They deleted the tree ring data from the 1960s and spliced in the thermometer data and smoothed the two to disguise the join. Simple! And, of course, deeply wrong.

It begs the question, if tree rings do not capture current temperatures, can they be relied on to be a proxy for past temperatures? There is another question. If the scientific consensus thinks it is acceptable to manipulate data that is presented to the public in this way then what other tricks are they hiding?

The problem of divining past temperatures does not answer the main question whether we should be concerned about CO_2 emissions and their possible effect of warming the planet to a dangerous degree. Sadly for alarmists, there is another major problem with the unprecedented warming narrative. It's called 'The Pause'.

TREEMOMETERS

Over 50 flavours!
PAUSE
EXCUSE CHOCS
OOo.. I'M GETTING OCEAN BREEZE WITH HINT OF NATURAL PINE AND ... AND ... IT'S JUST THE HEAT THAT'S MISSING
EVERY EXCUSE UNDER THE SUN
(EXCEPT THE SUN)
JOSH '14
FATTEN UP YOUR GRANT!

The Science – The Pause

There was no significant increase in temperature for nearly 20 years between the late 90s and 2015. It may be warmer than it was 100 years ago, but global temperatures have not increased much, if at all, since the turn of the century. Hence the term 'The Pause.' Even the recent record El Niño (2015/16) has not increased the warming trend alarmingly and temperatures have cooled again in the last few years.

Climate scientists have come up with all kinds of excuses for The Pause – well over 60 by the last count – and over 200 scientific papers have been written on the subject. The scientists themselves cannot agree, some saying The Pause does not actually exist and others saying it must be natural variation, or volcanoes, or that all the heat is has cleverly disappeared into the deep oceans without warming anything on the way down (and we cannot measure the temperature down there anyway).

A NOAA scientist, Tom Karl, famously adjusted the data to disappear The Pause just before the 2015 Paris Climate Conference. But a fellow NOAA scientist, Dr. John Bates, said of the paper '... the evidence kept mounting that Tom Karl constantly had his 'thumb on the scale' – in the documentation, scientific choices, and release of datasets – in an effort to discredit the notion of a global warming hiatus and rush to time the publication of the paper to influence national and international deliberations on climate policy.'

How about the weather. Surely that shows signs of climate change?

The UK Met Office receive £millions to build computer models to create alarming predictions which help them solicit even more millions... and so on. Models are, as the saying goes, always wrong but some are helpful – I am not sure that includes climate models. They are sometimes called GIGO – Garbage In, Garbage Out.

SOME THINGS DON'T CHANGE

The Science – Weather

Weather is frequently linked to climate change. If it's dry, it's climate change; if it's wet, it's climate change; if it's windy, it's climate change. Any kind of weather event is climate change, a storm, a flood, a heatwave. As George Monbiot, *Guardian* journalist and environmentalist, explained recently to female reader, even freezing cold weather is due to global warming. Convenient.

CAUGHT OUT IN THE COLD

GEORGE MAKING-IT-UP-AS-HE-GOES-ALONG-MONBIOT MANSPLAINS CLIMATE CHANGE

Talking of the activists, let's go global.

UN Climate Talks: The Ritual

UN climate talks follow well recognised stages. Everyone arrives at the conference with high hopes that this time things will be different, even though this is the Last Chance to Save the Planet. Emotional presentations are made and politicians join the chorus that Time is Running Out. Celebrities join in with the protesting activists. We then move to deadlock where individual nations cannot agree, usually about how much money they will gain or lose, followed by a breakthrough in the final extra hours of the conference. Finally everyone goes home realising that what they actually achieved was worthless.

The Politics – UN COP

The 'Conference of Parties', or COP, is a United Nations meeting of politicians and negotiators coming together to agree a global approach to carbon dioxide emissions and climate change – see opposite for how the conference ritual works.

The 19th COP in Copenhagen 2009, in the aftermath of Climategate, was a disaster for activists and alarmists and a victory for common sense and sceptics. COP21, in Paris 2015, was seen as a success by the organisers but not by the activists.

CHINESE WHISPERS

Politicians from around the world had managed to negotiate a non-binding agreement that sounded great but would do nothing – which looked a lot like every other COP. For the activists this was not an impressive step forward. It was, as James Hansen said, 'a fraud'.

TOLD YOU SO!

This would be a good point to talk about The Green Blob.

28GATE

WAYBACK WHEN
THEY DECIDED WHAT WE SHOULD THINK

In what became known as '28gate', the BBC tried to keep the list of seminar attendees (the 'best scientific experts') secret for years, spending thousands of pounds in the process. Happily Tony Newbery and Andrew Montford exposed the scandal and Maurizio Morabito discovered the list, which comprised of mostly green activists, just two climate scientists and only one dissenting voice.

The Green Blob – The BBC

'The Green Blob' is a term coined by Owen Paterson, MP and former UK Government environment secretary.

He defined the Green Blob as 'the mutually supportive network of environmental pressure groups, renewable energy companies and some public officials who keep each other well supplied with lavish funds, scare stories and green tape.'

The Green Blob includes the BBC. In 2006 a curious seminar took place where green activists lectured 28 senior BBC executives – see opposite.

Andrew Montford summarises in his report *The Propaganda Bureau*: 'In 2007, the BBC Trust announced that a seminar of the "best scientific experts"' had decided that climate science was settled and that dissenting voices no longer deserved equal treatment.' Andrew concludes 'The BBC's journalists and management have been using the corporation's vast resources to promote the views of green pressure groups'.

Aah, the Stench of Green Subsidies

The amount of money in subsidies and green finance is eye watering. The billions of dollars given to Elon Musk, for example, may indeed allow some very wealthy people to drive a superb electric car. But every taxpayer in the US has to pay for it.

In the US, renewable energy gets 25 times the subsidy that fossil fuels get, and the money goes to the producers not the consumers, whereas for fossil fuels the money goes to the consumers. So green finance and subsidies benefit the rich while fossil fuel subsidies benefit everyone, the poor benefiting the most, of course.

ONLY $4.9 BILLION

Below: why do Greens keep getting things wrong?

The Green Blob – The Greens

We all care about our environment. From air pollution, to plastic waste in our oceans and saving wilderness from excessive human development – we are all 'Green'. We want clean air and to preserve the wonderful planet we live on.

Organisations like Greenpeace or Friends of the Earth have been good at raising levels of public awareness of environmental issues. However, when it comes to wider issues, such as energy and farming, Green organisations have tended to lobby for policies that are harmful to people and the planet. From promoting 'renewable' energy, such as biofuels, to crusading against genetically modified foods, like Golden Rice, developed to combat Vitamin A deficiency, the policies promoted by Greens have been deadly.

For example, Biofuels have been promoted as a source of green, clean and renewable energy. But clearing ten million acres of Indonesian rain forest (which itself releases CO_2 emissions) for palm oil crops must raise questions as to what the terms as 'green', 'clean' and 'renewable' actually mean.

50 SHADES OF GREEN

But before we look at the darkest side of climate change alarmism let's take a look at some of the other key players in the whole debate. The scientists.

Bloggers, often retired scientists or engineers, are frequently more expert at analysing data than climate scientists. This is actually a great thing for the future of science.

The Scientists

Most scientists are happiest being left alone to do science. They have a tough time in the climate change debate, with activists and politicians demanding they communicate terrifying alarmist messages. They are often not skilled or interested in this type of communication. Typically science is understated and uncertain, couched in careful language, making any 'political' statements look less than persuasive.

NEW TIPPING POINT DISCOVERED

So on the one hand they are given research grants by governments to show how global warming is 'real, manmade and happening' and then hounded for soundbites by activists, some of whom, just to confuse everyone, might be a fellow scientists.

SIGNS OF THE TIMES

Cue the villains of climate alarmism.

CLIMATE OLYMPICS

All the kind of activities that make Michael Mann the climate science expert he is today.

The Climate Cast

The decidedly heated atmosphere of the climate debate has given us a cast of colourful characters on both sides of the debate.

Michael Mann is clearly a favourite and the subject of many cartoons. He is the main instigator of the infamous Hockey Stick graph and the subject of Mark Steyn's entertaining and excoriating book *A Disgrace to the Profession*. In 2019 Mann lost his lawsuit against Tim Ball, who was awarded costs, because Mann failed to share his data.

Gavin Schmidt looks like Michael Mann's twin. While he is fully on board the alarmist train, he is a solid communicator and engages with almost everyone in the climate debate. Right is *Vintage Gavin*, fitting data to fit a story. I drew the cartoon after he pointed out how few English vineyards there were in medieval times (46 were recorded in the Domesday Book – ironic name) compared to the present day, over 400. What he neglected to note was the population of England was, at around 2 million, less than a thirtieth of what it is today. So we should really have 1518 vineyards!

SPONGE BOB SMEAR PANTS

Other dubious characters include many so-called 'climate communicators' who do just the opposite. They will harangue you on blogs, and troll or block you on Twitter, for asking the wrong question, breathing or having a view that is not 100% pure alarmist. Recently I heard about a collection of Twitter 'block lists' which allow you to automatically block 54,000 'climate incorrect' accounts on Twitter. The list includes not just climate sceptics but anyone who questions the alarmist narrative, even highly respective climate scientists such as Dr Roger Pielke Jr.

Bob Ward, above, is an infamous spinner and smearer in the UK, employed by the Grantham Institute, and who attacks anyone on the sceptic side of the debate.

MONTFORD REPLIES WITH STELLAR BACK UP

(DR JUDITH CURRY RECOMMENDS THE HOCKEY STICK ILLUSION)

"ON THE SAME TEAM"
PR UPDATE

Climate Heroes

Climate heroes are those either side of the debate who stick up for science, who don't give way to unscientific beliefs or alarmism and who sometimes take career threatening risks in doing so.

Our first and foremost climate hero is climate scientist Judith Curry – her ability to articulate the science in a reasoned level-headed way is impressive. She is, for me, one of the most reliable sources of insight and balance in the whole debate. She is recently retired and the former chair of the School of Earth and Atmospheric Sciences at the Georgia Institute of Technology. She is highly intelligent, honest and runs a lively blog called Climate Etc.

JUDITH CURRY PATRON SAINT OF CLIMATE SCIENCE THROWS DOWN THE GAUNTLET

Other climate heroes are legion.

Various heroes, from top left: Anthony Watts; Steve McIntyre, Andrew Montford; Lucia Liljegren; Donna Laframboise. Below: Richard Betts, Ed Hawkins and Tamsin Edwards.

THE PAUSE ~ NOT BREAKING ANY SPEED LIMITS

I seem to have met a huge number of exceptional people on both sides of the debate. First, some sceptical heroes of the climate blogosphere: notably Anthony Watts, Watts Up With That blog; Steven McIntyre, Climate Audit blog; Andrew Montford; Roger Pielke Jr and Sr, and Roy Spencer at their respective blogs; Donna Laframboise, No Frakking Consensus blog; Jo Nova, at her blog; Roger Tattersall, Tallbloke's Talkshop blog; Paul Homewood, Not A Lot of People Know That blog; Lucia Liljegren, at the Rank Exploits/Blackboard blog.

In the UK there are a number of hero journalists: James Delingpole is a must-read on climate; as are Matt Ridley, Christopher Booker and David Rose. In the US, Mark Steyn and Alex Epstein have been prominent writers in the debate. Internationally Bjorn Lomborg is one of the most respected voices.

THE CANUCK SHOWS HOW TO USE A HOCKEY STICK
Mark Steyn at the Senate

There are also heroes on the less sceptical side, for example Richard Betts of the Met Office, Ed Hawkins of Reading University and Tamsin Edwards of the Open University, all heroes to me for their civility and openness to discussion. I also have a soft spot for Leo Hickman of Carbon Brief and George Monbiot of the UK *Guardian* newspaper. I know some will consider them more zero than hero but at least they don't block me on Twitter... yet.

I have missed dozens of names from all over the globe – I apologise unreservedly. I am sure you know who you are.

Now to the really serious problems.

'GREENING' THE LAND

Above: wind turbines needs fossil fuel back up for the times the wind does not blow or it blows too much. Why double your infrastructure and destabalise your electricity grid, all for some virtue signalling 'bird slicing bat chomping eco-crucifixes'?

Right: This was drawn in 2012 and since then world wind energy may well be above 0% but not much.

There is nothing good about giant wind turbines. They are bad for the environment, bad for the economy, bad for the poor. Bad. There may be smaller turbines or other turbine designs that may be useful in certain off grid situations but they are certainly not the panacea they are made out to be.

ALL THE PAIN FOR ZERO GAIN

PAINFUL FACTS ABOUT WIND ENERGY

WIND TURBINES KILL BIRDS

THEY ALSO KILL BATS

THEY ARE BUILT IN AREAS OF OUTSTANDING NATURAL BEAUTY

THEY ARE NOISY

THEY REQUIRE PERMANENT FOSSIL FUEL BACK UP

THEY USE PRECIOUS RARE EARTH MINERALS

THEY LEAD TO FOREST CLEARING

1 EXPENSIVE 'GREEN' JOB LEADS TO 3.7 JOB LOSSES

'GREEN' TAXES CONTRIBUTE TO FUEL POVERTY

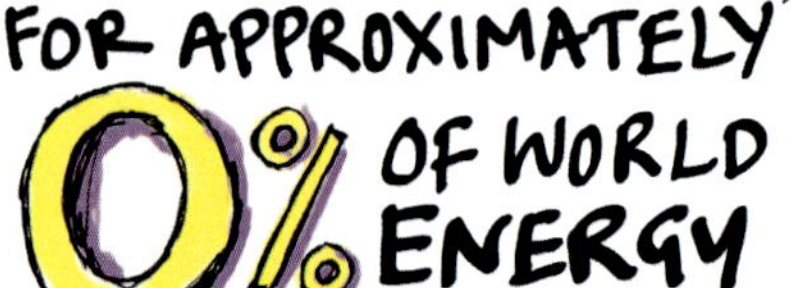

So what's the Big Deal?

We can see why the subject of climate change is controversial. One side is arguing that the science is unequivocal: mankind is causing dangerous catastrophic climate change, the biggest threat to Planet Earth ever. The other side says the science is hugely uncertain and the greatest scam of modern times is being foisted on western civilisation by left-wing activists and politicians. Who is right?

If this was simply a scientific debate I think we could safely wait and see how it plays out. The real problem is the imagined risks of climate change versus the real impacts of climate change policy.

Here's an example: giant wind turbines - see left for a summary. They are the most expensive and grotesque folly of our day. They are an appalling waste of money and technology. For some reason they are favoured by environmentalists, who seem happy to concrete over acres of countryside, kill eagles, bats and insects, produce meagre amounts of expensive intermittent electricity, destroy the environment, ruin beautiful countryside, and do almost nothing to decrease CO_2 emissions. They are knives in the sky and unreliable producers of electricity.

BE A SUPER HERO: FIGHT EVIL WIND

WIND TURBINES TO REDUCE BATS BY 90%

INFOTOON

BONKERS RENEWABLES

WITH HARD NUMBERS

PER YEAR!

IF WE DIDNT SPEND **\$23.8 BILLION** ON WIND

WE COULD SAVE **100 MILLION** BIRDS & BATS

THANKS!

PER YEAR!

IF WE DIDNT SPEND **\$35 BILLION** ON SOLAR

WE COULD SPEND MONEY ON HEALTH & SAVE **2.75 MILLION** ADULTS & CHILDREN

PER YEAR!

IF WE DIDNT SPEND **\$20 BILLION** ON BIOFUELS

WE COULD FEED **30 MILLION** HUNGRY PEOPLE

...AND HOW MUCH WOULD ALL THIS MONEY POSTPONE GLOBAL WARMING BY 2100?

1 DAY

ALL NUMBERS COME FROM COPENHAGEN CONSENSUS 2012 AND CALCULATIONS BY BJORN LOMBORG.
BIRD & BAT NUMBERS ARE FROM MARK DUCHAMP WWW.SAVETHEEAGLESINTERNATIONAL.ORG

Wind turbines are not the only problem, other renewables like solar panels and biofuels are expensive and have negative impacts too – some 'solar farms' concentrate solar light, frying birds in the process. Biofuels destroy our forests.

Green jobs are another of the supposed goals of spending money on renewables but if you lose many more jobs while doing so it is does not make much sense.

GREEN JOBS

SUSTAINABLE - BUT NOT FOR EVERYONE

Every green job costs three other jobs

The huge sums of money on renewable energy mean we cannot spend it on other things, like affordable health care and education, or eradicating poverty. These are real problems affecting the world, especially the poor, right now.

The billions of dollars spent on renewables, as Bjorn Lomborg has worked out, would prevent a whole day of global warming between now and 2100. One day. All in all it's just not worth it.

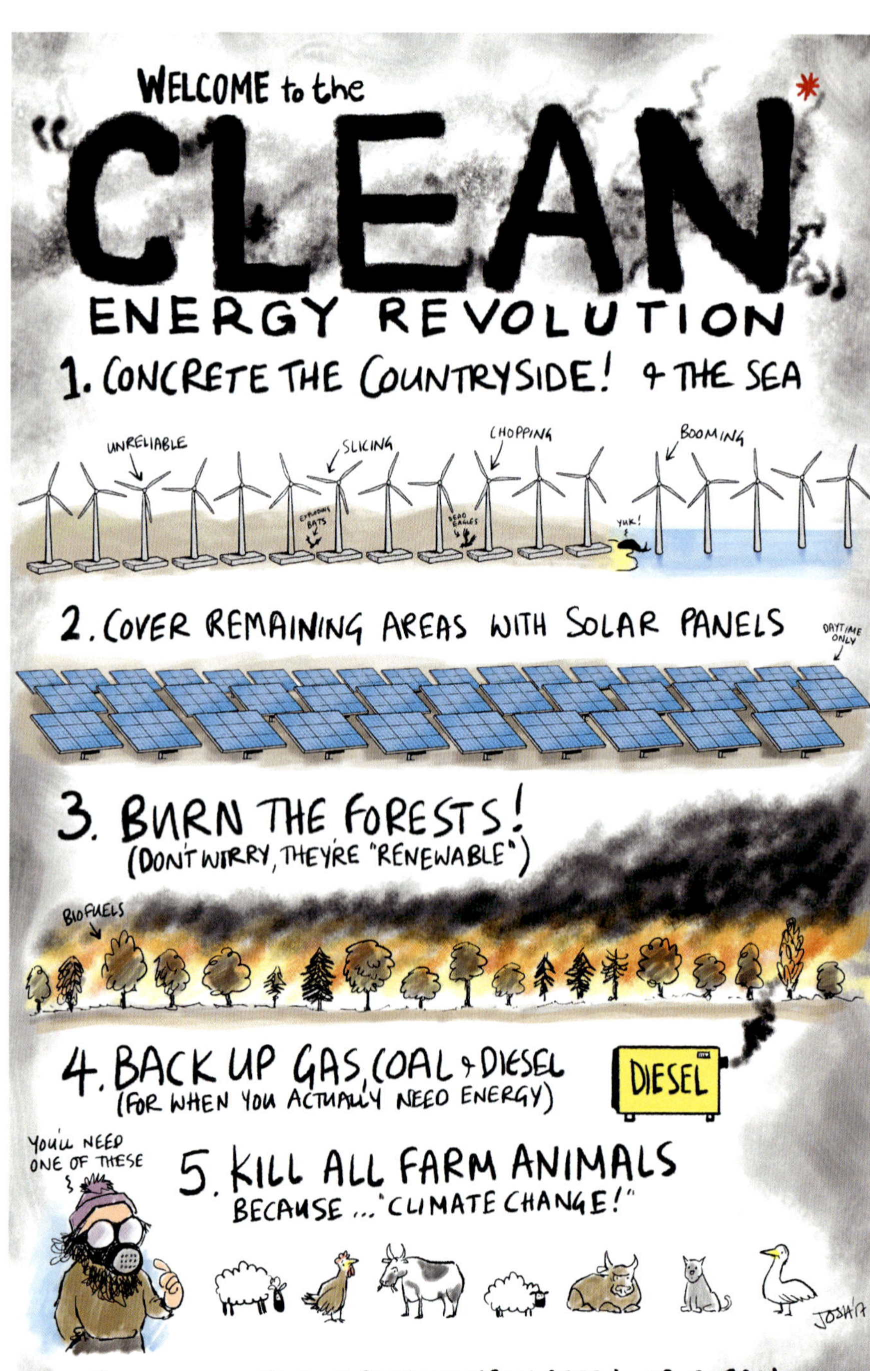
WELCOME to the
"CLEAN"*
ENERGY REVOLUTION
1. CONCRETE THE COUNTRYSIDE! & THE SEA
UNRELIABLE
SLICING
CHOPPING
BOOMING
EXPLODING BATS
DEAD EAGLES
YUK!
2. COVER REMAINING AREAS WITH SOLAR PANELS
DAYTIME ONLY
3. BURN THE FORESTS!
(DON'T WORRY, THEY'RE "RENEWABLE")
BIOFUELS
4. BACK UP GAS, COAL & DIESEL
(FOR WHEN YOU ACTUALLY NEED ENERGY)
DIESEL
YOU'LL NEED ONE OF THESE
5. KILL ALL FARM ANIMALS
BECAUSE ... "CLIMATE CHANGE!"
JOSH '17
*PLEASE NOTE: "CLEAN" DOES NOT MEAN GREEN... OR CLEAN

Dark Times

You might well say 'So what if there is uncertainty, cost and sacrifice? If we create a better, safer, healthier, sustainable, more environmentally friendly world then it will all have been worth it.' Surely this is a slam dunk argument – no contest, right? Game over, sceptics!

But here is the problem – the opposite is happening.

Environmentalism and especially renewables, as we have already seen, are not saving the planet. They are killing people and destroying the environment. Renewables are not cleaner, healthier or more sustainable – they are the opposite.

Biofuels, where we emit just as much CO_2 as before, destroy forests, even supposedly protected ones (see next page) and cause food price rises, leading to hunger and land grabs. Or the smog in our cities – how much has the promotion of diesel vehicles or wood burning stoves contributed to this?

CO_2 is not a pollutant. It is an odourless, colourless gas necessary for life on this planet. The very survival of the biosphere depends on CO_2. The exhaust fumes from diesel vehicles and the smoke from burning wood do contain pollutants that affect our health but CO_2 is not one of them.

Do we really have to mitigate against feeling a bit concerned about the future? And why are we cutting down protected forests to burn wood?

The VW diesel emissions scandal exposed another insane Green nightmare: the promotion of a dirty fuel as good for the environment.

We pay for all this 'clean' renewable energy to avoid so called climate change impacts. But are there any catastrophic anthropogenic climate impacts? From hurricanes (no increase) to 'The Pause', the present warming climate does not seem catastrophic. Sea levels have been rising for thousands of years and with no acceleration in the rate and no link to CO_2 from burning fossil fuels.

Only computer climate models project an alarming future. Actual evidence points to a different conclusion. Yes, of course, if the planet became a superhot sauna or a freezing snowball then life would be very difficult, but no one is predicting such extremes – not even the models.

Some invoke an idea called the Precautionary Principle and say we should do something 'just in case', like an insurance policy (shouldn't we be 'precautious' about using the Precautionary Principle?). But politicians and environmentalists are buying the wrong policies. They favour energy generation that is too expensive and unreliable. The only realistic 'carbon neutral' source of energy is nuclear, and while it is expensive at the moment it is the best long-term answer if the aim is to reduce CO_2 emissions from burning fossil fuels. Instead we have the disastrous example of Germany's energy policy, 'Energiewende', where they have closed nuclear power plants in favour of coal, wind and solar. It has taken Angela Merkel to the cliff edge and soon will take her over it.

So is there any hope for the future? Yes, there fracking well is.

THE SHALE GAS REVOLUTION

Fracking the Future

Fracking is the future – as is nuclear energy. Fracking is a revolution happening right now across the globe: cheap, accessible and abundant energy, giving independence of energy supply back to nations, small companies, small operators and local economies. It could, where it is allowed, truly democratise energy supply. Less OPEC and Russia, more county and shire.

First lets look at the benefits. One: you only need one little tap.

FRACT SHEET No.2

TIME TO FRACK? 3 DAYS

DRILLING THE WELL: 1 MONTH

FRACKING THE WELL: 3 DAYS

OIL OR GAS PRODUCTION: 10 – 20 YEARS

FRACT SHEET No.3

HOW DEEP IS THAT DRILL?

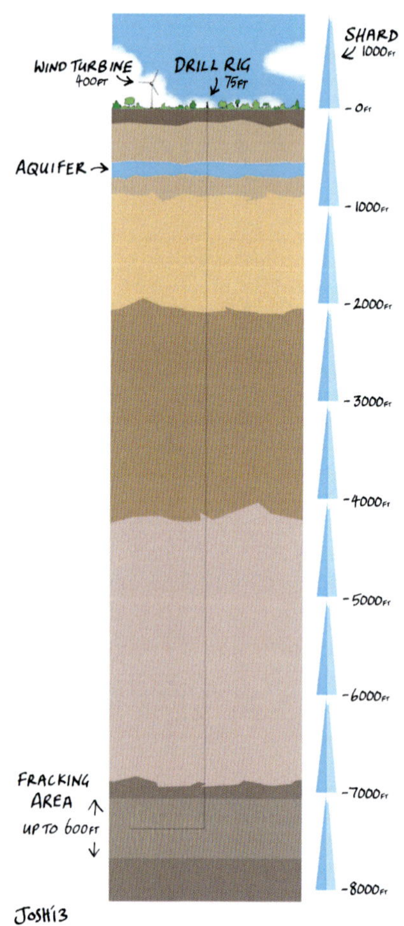

JOSH'13

Fracking seems to have the added 'benefit' of reducing CO_2 emissions. To the great dismay of many international alarmists, the United States, no longer supporting the Paris Climate Accord, has seen the most dramatic reduction in CO_2 emissions. This hardly seems fair when other countries have, for years, been relying on wind turbines and solar panels to reduce their own emissions with marginal success. Another country which has seen a large reduction in emissions is Russia – another large gas producer.

Two: the actual disruptive messy fracking bit lasts for a few months.

Three: the actual source of shale is a long way from the water table. So it won't contaminate our water.

Four: you can frack nearly everywhere and it is safe. Don't believe the Russian backed scaremongering.

The worst thing about fracking seems to be the protesters, as residents of Balcombe, Surrey UK, found. In protesting about fracking the protesters generally trashed the village and were much more disruptive than any drilling would be.

GET THE MESSAGE OUT

On a global stage fracking has already had an effect on oil prices and is likely to continue to do so. As I write the oil price is around $70 a barrel, which must be a good thing for the people that need affordable energy the most – those in the developing world and the poor.

The low oil price might be less good for large corporations or oil-rich countries that like to monopolise the energy market and maintain high costs. I don't find this very troubling.

We have sufficient problems in the world right now – war, hunger, disease, poverty, injustice – to keep us fully focused. One of our major problems, extreme poverty, is taking time and money to eradicate but it is happening.

Much of the 'alarm' about climate change is that all these problems, at some far distant time in the future, will get much worse – there will be 'climate refugees', more floods, more droughts, more storms, if we don't 'do something'. But what should that 'something' be when we have no idea if the climate will 'pause' or get colder or warmer? What if funding current climate mitigation simply exacerbates the suffering now?

However, I believe there is a lot to be hopeful about. So let's end with some optimism.

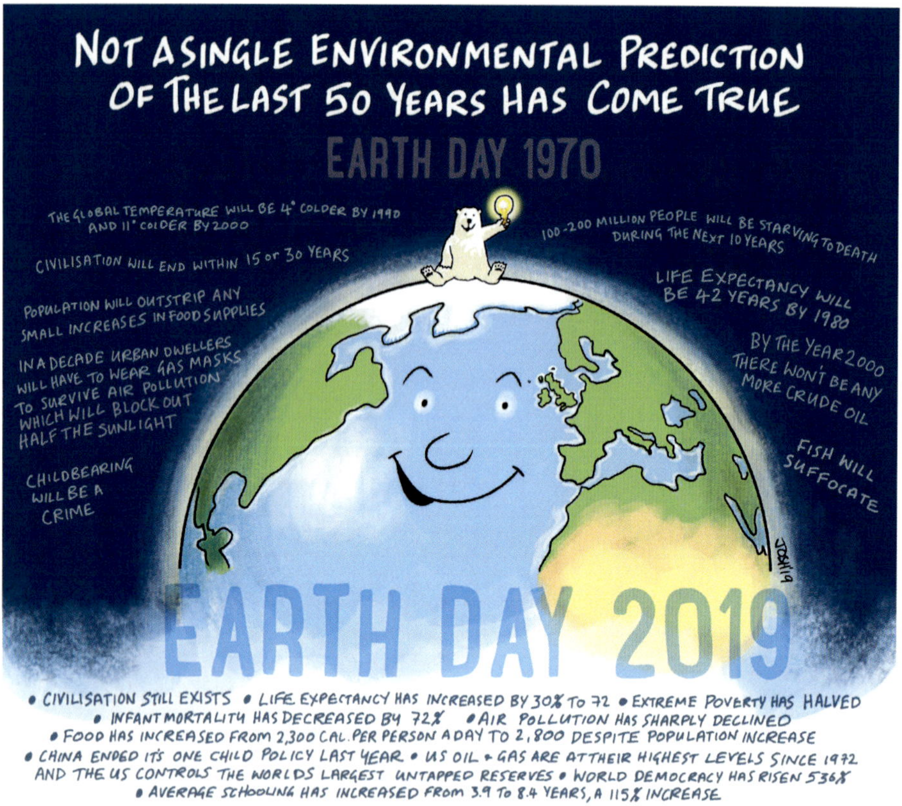

NOT A SINGLE ENVIRONMENTAL PREDICTION OF THE LAST 50 YEARS HAS COME TRUE

EARTH DAY 1970

THE GLOBAL TEMPERATURE WILL BE 4° COLDER BY 1990 AND 11° COLDER BY 2000

CIVILISATION WILL END WITHIN 15 OR 30 YEARS

POPULATION WILL OUTSTRIP ANY SMALL INCREASES IN FOOD SUPPLIES

IN A DECADE URBAN DWELLERS WILL HAVE TO WEAR GAS MASKS TO SURVIVE AIR POLLUTION WHICH WILL BLOCK OUT HALF THE SUNLIGHT

CHILDBEARING WILL BE A CRIME

100-200 MILLION PEOPLE WILL BE STARVING TO DEATH DURING THE NEXT 10 YEARS

LIFE EXPECTANCY WILL BE 42 YEARS BY 1980

BY THE YEAR 2000 THERE WON'T BE ANY MORE CRUDE OIL

FISH WILL SUFFOCATE

JOSH '19

EARTH DAY 2019

• CIVILISATION STILL EXISTS • LIFE EXPECTANCY HAS INCREASED BY 30% TO 72 • EXTREME POVERTY HAS HALVED • INFANT MORTALITY HAS DECREASED BY 72% • AIR POLLUTION HAS SHARPLY DECLINED • FOOD HAS INCREASED FROM 2,300 CAL. PER PERSON A DAY TO 2,800 DESPITE POPULATION INCREASE • CHINA ENDED IT'S ONE CHILD POLICY LAST YEAR • US OIL + GAS ARE AT THEIR HIGHEST LEVELS SINCE 1972 AND THE US CONTROLS THE WORLDS LARGEST UNTAPPED RESERVES • WORLD DEMOCRACY HAS RISEN 536% • AVERAGE SCHOOLING HAS INCREASED FROM 3.9 TO 8.4 YEARS, A 115% INCREASE

A Happy Ending?

There are many signs our climate is not changing very fast and unlikely to be dangerous. None of the doom-laden predictions from the last 50 years have come true - see left. We still have summer sea ice in the Arctic and sea levels, which have been rising for twenty thousand years, show no sign of a CO_2 impact.

It even looks like the theory of global warming driven by CO_2 emissions is incorrect. A more recent theory that fits observations better is that the sun regulates climate through cycles of its magnetic field and cosmic rays, the sub-atomic particles created by super nova. I am sure we will learn more in the coming years.

There are signs that scientists are getting fed up with activists hijacking the science. The more I listen to scientists the less concerned I am. This is partly because they are cautious about predicting catastrophe but it is also due to the plethora of scientific blogs. Now when an alarmist scare story hits the news headlines it can quickly be debunked. Bloggers rapidly test scientific papers and assess them for mistakes so corrections can be made. This kind of 'blog peer review' helps science become much more robust and reliable, open, transparent and credible.

Above: a similar theme as at the start of the book, it looks like we are turning into a world of sceptics. Many polls now do not even mention climate change as a major concern.

Right: there is even hope for The Pope.

The truth to title of this book, *All you need to know about Climate Change*, is that there is very little to know. Our amazing life-giving climate is still a mystery, and we don't know what will happen in the next five, ten, twenty or hundred years. Climate science provides few answers we can trust and the climate is not in 'crisis' or in an 'emergency'.

So the final cartoon in this book is the image of a happy planet. There are many reasons to be optimistic despite the problems we still have to overcome.

Climate change may be one of them, but not quite yet.

A DOZEN REASONS TO BE CHEERFUL
(FOR LOTS MORE SEE 'THE RATIONAL OPTIMIST' BY MATT RIDLEY)

Drawn for Tony Heller at Realclimatescience.com blog

Appendix: References and notes

There are many excellent blogs out there, and thousands of pages and scientific papers that are available online. The list here are those which are relevant to the text in this book. They are also online at www.cartoonsbyjosh.com/booklinks.

Sheep Mountain
http://climateaudit.org/2014/12/04/sheep-mountain-update/

Hockey stick
http://joannenova.com.au/2009/12/fraudulent-hockey-sticks-and-hidden-data/

http://notrickszone.com/2013/10/17/climatology-sees-one-of-the-greatest-scientific-reversals-of-all-time-the-rise-and-fall-of-the-hockey-stick-charts/

Climategate Inquiries
http://www.parliament.uk/business/committees/committees-archive/science-technology/s-t-cru-inquiry/

The Pause
http://hockeyschtick.blogspot.com/2014/11/updated-list-of-64-excuses-for-18-26.html

The Green Blob
http://www.telegraph.co.uk/news/politics/10978678/Owen-Paterson-Im-proud-of-standing-up-to-the-green-lobby.html

GMO
http://www.telegraph.co.uk/news/earth/greenpolitics/11427506/Owen-Paterson-the-Green-Blob-is-threatening-lives-in-Africa.html

Golden Rice
https://en.wikipedia.org/wiki/Golden_rice and http://goldenrice.org

28gate
http://bishophill.squarespace.com/blog/2012/11/19/orlowski-why-28gate-matters.html

BBC
http://www.thegwpf.org/images/stories/gwpf-reports/booker-bbc.pdf

Judith Curry and the Precautionary principle
http://judithcurry.com/2016/01/05/climate-models-and-precautionary-measures/

Fracking in Balcombe
http://www.bishop-hill.net/blog/2013/8/13/balcombe-parish-chairman-tells-protestors-to-frack-off.html

http://www.bishop-hill.net/blog/2013/8/13/an-epistle-from-balcombe-josh-234.html

English Vineyards
http://www.realclimate.org/index.php/archives/2006/11/english-vineyards-again/

John Bates at Climate Etc
https://judithcurry.com/2017/02/04/climate-scientists-versus-climate-data/

Bullying of Climate Scientitsts
https://wattsupwiththat.com/2014/05/16/ridley-on-the-bullying-of-climate-skeptics/

The famous VS thread at Bart's blog *(see left)*
http://ourchangingclimate.wordpress.com/2010/03/01/global-average-temperature-increase-giss-hadcru-and-ncdc-compared/#comments

Sea Ice
https://wattsupwiththat.com/reference-pages/sea-ice-page/

THE PRESENCE OF A UNIT ROOT

Antarctic Record Sea Ice
https://www.thegwpf.com/the-west-antarctic-ice-sheet-collapse/

Strong Arctic Sea Ice Growth
https://wattsupwiththat.com/2019/02/24/strong-arctic-sea-ice-growth-this-year/

Antarctic Peninsula cooling by almost 1 degree
http://joannenova.com.au/2017/04/there-goes-that-scare-antarctic-peninsula-cooling-by-almost-1-degree/

Medieval Warm Period
http://www.co2science.org/data/mwp/mwpp.php

The Skeptics Handbook
http://jonova.s3.amazonaws.com/sh1/the_skeptics_handbook_2-3_lq.pdf
http://jonova.s3.amazonaws.com/sh2/the_skeptics_handbook_IIj-sml.pdf

The Scientific Method
https://wattsupwiththat.com/2014/05/23/friday-funny-the-scientific-method/

Michael Mann loses lawsuit
https://wattsupwiththat.com/2019/08/22/breaking-dr-tim-ball-wins-michaelemann-lawsuit-mann-has-to-pay/

Climategate - The Breaking News Story, November 19th 2009
https://wattsupwiththat.com/2009/11/19/breaking-news-story-hadley-cru-has-apparently-been-hacked-hundreds-of-files-released/ (and https://wattsupwiththat.com/climategate/)

Good reads

Like the blogs there is so much worth reading on climate change and energy. The list below is simply those that have inspired some of the cartoons in this book.

The Hockey Stick Illusion by Andrew Montford.
https://www.amazon.co.uk/Hockey-Stick-Illusion-W-Montford/dp/0957313527/

The Rational Optimist by Matt Ridley
https://www.amazon.co.uk/Rational-Optimist-How-Prosperity-Evolves/dp/0007267126

The Propaganda Bureau
https://www.amazon.co.uk/Propaganda-Bureau-W-Montford/dp/148123613X/

A Disgrace to the Profession by Mark Steyn
https://www.amazon.co.uk/Disgrace-Profession-Mark-Steyn-ebook/dp/B013TZFRGE/

The Moral Case for Fossil Fuels by Alex Epstein
https://www.amazon.co.uk/Moral-Case-Fossil-Fuels/dp/1591847443/

Prominent climatologist Hubert Lamb and the transformation of climate science
https://www.thegwpf.org/content/uploads/2015/02/Lamb.pdf

Activist Facts: Greenpeace
https://www.activistfacts.com/organizations/131-greenpeace/

The Climategate emails – a booklet
http://www.lavoisier.com.au/articles/greenhouse-science/climate-change/climategate-emails.pdf

The Chilling Stars: A Cosmic View of Climate Change
https://www.amazon.co.uk/Chilling-Stars-New-Theory-Climate/dp/1840468661

Watermelons by James Delingpole
https://www.amazon.co.uk/Watermelons-Environmentalists-Destroying-Stealing-Childrens/dp/1849544050/

Green Tyranny by Rupert Darwall
https://www.amazon.co.uk/Green-Tyranny-Exposing-Totalitarian-Industrial/dp/1641770449

The Little Green Book of Eco-Fascism: The Plan to Frighten Your Kids, Drive Up Energy Costs and Hike Your Taxes! by James Delingpole
https://www.amazon.co.uk/Little-Green-Book-Eco-Fascism-Frighten/dp/1849546355

Download the ClimateGate email archive
https://www.enlightenedtechnology.org/download-the-leaked-climate-gate-email-archive/

Good views

Some links to online videos

Did we ever have a debate?

'Global Warming Is Not A Crisis', a debate hosted by Intelligence Squared. Spoiler: 'Not a crisis won'. Watch it on YouTube https://www.youtube.com/watch?v=f-28qNd6ass

Nuclear

Why renewables can't save the planet by Michael Shellenberger
https://www.youtube.com/watch?v=N-yALPEpV4w

Accompanying article in Quilette
https://twitter.com/ShellenbergerMD/status/1101144047874273280?s=20

https://www.ted.com/talks/michael_shellenberger_how_fear_of_nuclear_power_is_hurting_the_environment

Talks at Google - The Moral Case for Fossil Fuels - Alex Epstein
https://www.youtube.com/watch?v=s6b7K1hjZk4

The Rubin Report - Is There Still a Debate Over Climate Change with Alex Epstein
https://www.youtube.com/watch?v=yJmL9hRrplQ

The letter from Mr FOIA (Freedom of Information Act) who leaked the ClimateGate emails:

It's time to tie up loose ends and dispel some of the speculation surrounding the Climategate affair.

Indeed, it's singular "I" this time. After certain career developments I can no longer use the papal plural.

If this email seems slightly disjointed it's probably my linguistic background and the problem of trying to address both the wider audience (I expect this will be partially reproduced sooner or later) and the email recipients (whom I haven't decided yet on).

The "all.7z" password is [redacted] DO NOT PUBLISH THE PASSWORD. Quote other parts if you like.

Releasing the encrypted archive was a mere practicality. I didn't want to keep the emails lying around.

I prepared CG1 & 2 [previous email releases] alone. Even skimming through all 220.000 emails would have taken several more months of work in an increasingly unfavorable environment.

Dumping them all into the public domain would be the last resort. Majority of the emails are irrelevant, some of them probably sensitive and socially damaging.

To get the remaining scientifically (or otherwise) relevant emails out, I ask you to pass this on to any motivated and responsible individuals who could volunteer some time to sift through the material for eventual release.

Filtering\redacting personally sensitive emails doesn't require special expertise.

I'm not entirely comfortable sending the password around unsolicited, but haven't got better ideas at the moment. If you feel this makes you seemingly "complicit" in a way you don't like, don't take action.

I don't expect these remaining emails to hold big surprises. Yet it's possible that the most important pieces are among them. Nobody on the planet has held the archive in plaintext since CG2.

That's right; no conspiracy, no paid hackers, no Big Oil. The Republicans didn't plot this. USA politics is alien to me, neither am I from the UK. There is life outside the Anglo-American sphere.

If someone is still wondering why anyone would take these risks, or sees only a breach of privacy here, a few words...

The first glimpses I got behind the scenes did little to garner my trust in the state of climate science — on the contrary. I found myself in front of a choice that just might have a global impact.

Briefly put, when I had to balance the interests of my own safety, privacy\career of a few scientists, and the well-being of billions of people living in the coming several decades, the first two weren't the decisive concern.

It was me or nobody, now or never. Combination of several rather improbable prerequisites just wouldn't occur again for anyone else in the foreseeable future. The circus was about to arrive in Copenhagen. Later on it could be too late.

Most would agree that climate science has already directed where humanity puts its capability, innovation, mental and material "might". The scale will grow ever grander in the coming decades if things go according to script. We're dealing with $trillions and potentially drastic influence on practically everyone.

Wealth of the surrounding society tends to draw the major brushstrokes of a newborn's future life. It makes a huge difference whether humanity uses its assets to achieve progress, or whether it strives to stop and reverse it, essentially sacrificing the less fortunate to the climate gods.

We can't pour trillions in this massive hole-digging-and-filling-up endeavor and pretend it's not away from something and someone else.

If the economy of a region, a country, a city, etc. deteriorates, what happens among the poorest? Does that usually improve their prospects? No, they will take the hardest hit. No amount of magical climate thinking can turn this one upside-down.

It's easy for many of us in the western world to accept a tiny green inconvenience and then wallow in that righteous feeling, surrounded by our "clean" technology and energy that is only slightly more expensive if adequately subsidized.

Those millions and billions already struggling with malnutrition, sickness, violence, illiteracy, etc. don't have that luxury. The price of "climate protection" with its cumulative and collateral effects is bound to destroy and debilitate in great numbers, for decades and generations.

Conversely, a "game-changer" could have a beneficial effect encompassing a similar scope.

If I had a chance to accomplish even a fraction of that, I'd have to try. I couldn't morally afford inaction. Even if I risked everything, would never get personal compensation, and could probably never talk about it with anyone.

I took what I deemed the most defensible course of action, and would do it again (although with slight alterations — trying to publish something truthful on RealClimate was clearly too grandiose of a plan ;-). [Note:RealClimate.org is an alarmist blog site co-founded by Michael Mann, a key Climategate figure and author of a flawed "hockey stick" graph which suggested that human CO_2 emissions are leading to a global warming catastrophe.]

Even if I have it all wrong and these scientists had some good reason to mislead us (instead of making a strong case with real data) I think disseminating the truth is still the safest bet by far.

Big thanks to Steve and Anthony and many others. My contribution would never have happened without your work (whether or not you agree with the views stated).

Oh, one more thing. I was surprised to learn from a "progressive" blog, corroborated by a renowned "scientist", that the releases were part of a coordinated campaign receiving vast amounts of secret funding from shady energy industry groups.

I wasn't aware of the arrangement but warmly welcome their decision to support my project. For that end I opened a bitcoin address: 1HHQ36qbsgGZWLPmiUjYHxQUPJ6EQXVJFS.

More seriously speaking, I accept, with gratitude, modest donations to support The (other) Cause. The address can also serve as a digital signature to ward off those identity thefts which are part of climate scientists' repertoire of tricks these days.

Keep on the good work. I won't be able to use this email address for long so if you reply, I can't guarantee reading or answering. I will [send] several batches, to anyone I can think of.

Over and out.

Mr. FOIA

Online: https://www.forbes.com/sites/larrybell/2013/03/15/who-released-the-climategate-emails-and-why/#2377d8fe40e5

Acknowledgements

Many thanks to Andrew Montford for his inspiring writing and blogging, and in helping put this book together. Thanks too to the many other bloggers, especially Anthony Watts, Steve McIntyre and Judith Curry, as well all those who comment on their blogs or on Twitter. They inspire, challenge and give brilliant feedback. The cartoons were originally drawn for them.

A special thanks to Benny Peiser, Director of the Global Warming Policy Foundation, whose support over the years has been greatly appreciated. Also special thanks to Matt Ridley who helped make this book possible.

Thanks to the journalists James Delingpole and others, who, like Christopher Booker, have written so entertainingly and dared to go against the prevailing doomsday narrative in mainstream newspapers. They have given sceptics a voice where otherwise there would only be wailing and tooth-gnashing of alarmist activists. I'd also like to thank Richard Betts, of the Met Office, a climate scientist willing to engage politely with sceptics – a rare thing. He frequently inspires cartoons as a result.

I should also mention Lyndsey Ward whose stories about Wind turbines, *Subsidy Sam* and *Tiny the Turbine*, I have illustrated – thank you, Lyndsey.

Thanks too to the many people I have met along the way who have inspired the cartoons and to all those who I have connected with via social media or who have donated or bought calendars, again, thank you all!

Josh
www.cartoonsbyjosh.com